Dahi Tamara Koch

Within the Event Horizon

poetry & prose

Bibliografische Information der Deutschen Nationalbibliothek: Die Deutsche Nationalbibliothek verzeichnet diese Publikation in der Deutschen Nationalbibliografie; detaillierte bibliografische Daten sind im Internet über dnb.dnb.de abrufbar.

© 2019 Dahi Tamara Koch
E-Mail: strangenessandcharms@email.de
Internet: www.strangeness-and-charms.com
Cover, translation and design by Dahi Tamara Koch, Baden-Baden, Germany
Copy editing by Phil Dragash
Printed and published by BoD – Books on Demand, Norderstedt.

ISBN: 9783749495719

Saturn

I'm grown up -
why should I believe in fairytales

vast lands
and a horizon
near my fingertips

nearly touching the skies
I see my earth at a distance

neither in field
nor in flower
will I grasp my tomorrow

no water
offers the solution
I need to drink

I'm full of words I cannot take hold of
my pen children keep silent

ever since I met you
my heart cannot retire

consciously
I misread myself
in you

I opened up
like a book

and innocence
turned the page

but you remain
the book of seven seals

unconsciously
tearing my pages apart

feeling like December
acting like Summer

now dream, forgotten
in the somnambulist's sleep
my solid sensation
hacked and picked

and innocence slipped away
buried
in a kiss of life

eyes like fairytales

you don't believe in

whenever you go
the heavens shed the tears
I'm not able to weep

for a moment I stood still
in your arms
but I kept on running

for a moment you stole
a forbidden glance from me

but you shall never be a part of my world –
I am his, and he is mine

I won't ever make room
for a second glance
between us

silent lies become a whispered truth
as my misery fades
like a symphony, coloured in blue

my heart still answering to your echo
lingering in this body of mine

don't you hide your soul away
don't you keep it in disguise

this heart of mine –
it doesn't compromise

mutual indifference

I like the way you keep the silence

and all the stitches in my heart

sometimes the silence

makes an overwhelming noise

we met
in a night without a morning –
silence echoed
in our hearts

I felt empty – my love drew to a close.
Now it's up to you to show me something –
if you have anything to show.

If it is love, it isn't destined
for silence.

We collected the cats on the riverbanks
and danced through the supermarket.
We counted the lights in the distance
and wrote our melodies on the wind.

Chocolate dreams were your gift
to all of my strawberry kisses.

So much warmth – even in the coldest of days.

[...] I'm missing us.

How am I supposed to feel if I don't know?

How am I supposed to know if I don't feel?

How am I supposed to feel what we are if doubt already whispers softly into my ears?

How should I think of us now if I dethink us in the past?

How am I supposed to talk to you if you cannot talk to me?

nostalgia makes the past dress up in prettier clothes
than those the present is wearing

we can live in none but the present

the past is past

the bygone days
cannot be filled with life

we are no time travellers

your idea of eternity

was too different from mine

A play of colours

Our beginning.
I see your blood, sweat and tears vibrate in every new day.

A breath of air in August.
The sound of the sea.
I can sense my solitude.

Feet stroke the grass.
I wander the woods, drink in the cedar trees.
I am with and within me.

The last hours of this very day paint the colours of kings
and queens on each and every wall.
Every treetop becomes a vespertine jewel.

Night.
Deep shadows in me and my soul
and a little black dress in my wardrobe.

Where are you?
Let us dance to the play of colours.
I can't feel them without you.

I sleep when I'm awake
and wake up when I'm asleep
never-ending night within me –
my songs fading away
on my muted lips

put your smile on my mouth
that dreams of you
kiss me awake
let my morning dawn

gift me the tomorrow
I cannot behold
for all I see is darkness

wandering around your head can never be wrong
but always beware of not losing your way

most love is lost in all that remains in the hidden

"When I think back to the first time we met, it feels like a dream," you said, only a few days later.
And thus you voiced what came true only a few months later.
It had been a dream.
[...]
"Even then, you have sealed our preterite," I said.
"Why do you say something like this," you asked me.
"Because we never had the chance to share the present."

hiding her axiom

in her heart's maze

songs that remind her of the childhood

she never had

wanting to change a person

who doesn't want to change himself

is like cosmetic surgery

on cancer patients

the blindest people think

they can see the most

summer storms –

poets let their souls fall down

like rain

the last words have been spoken
hanging over my head – the sword of Damocles
since the beginning of time

I will keep on weeping
over thoughts and over you
wandering about all of my rooms

your absence is all around me
and the silence is more frightening
then any sound has been before

too much is truth in those words:
that wonders are falsehood
and the days are gone, never to return

how blind can you be
with opened eyes

time after time
my demons leave me blind

and you walked into the night
and befriended the moon

when it's cold inside of me – tell me
who is keeping me warm

I need someone to hold me
to keep me warm at night
someone to fight my darkness
to bathe my world in light

I need someone who's near and
who's there to hold me tight
someone to tell me "Love, I
will never leave your side."

oh to be a dove

spreading its wings to fly far away

oh to just be free

to express all that I need to say

and thus I hid under the willow tree
its branches came and clung to
my arms and my cheek
and the heart that belonged to you

and I felt as if they whispered:
arbour maiden did your path lead you back to us

or was it a ghost, your ghost, that spoke from within them
reminding me of the love
we vowed in a long-gone May

it shall never be forgotten ...
I whispered

Love doesn't solely consist of books, films, and music and sharing the same past.

It consists of the present and the future.

It consists of the understanding that you want to grow and prosper together. That you don't solely look at each other but also look in the same direction.

We faced different directions, and it's no use to stick to that. We would waste away our time. We only live once. We're obliged to fill our time how we honestly, sincerely, want it to be.

My darling, sometimes love isn't enough.

Ours we have lost in a time in which both of us kept moving without looking at each other.

You will always be a part of me, and I will remain a part of you. You were a good chapter, but never more than that.

and we'll dance under moonlit skies

and we'll sing of ancient times

wait for me where the skies meet the sea

the otherworld where our old souls

will meet again for the very first time

where our imagination takes flight

and magic isn't a fairytale

I see the reflection of infinity

passing by my window

and the multitude of faceless guises

walking on water like shadows

Dethinking

I have to write.

I have to write and re-write myself in all that's hidden within me.

The unspoken heart is the place I need to travel to,

to rediscover the language that I had lost.

I felt and hoped myself empty in dreams that never belonged to me.

So how can I be with myself?

My heart struggled itself out of my body, lying shattered in pieces all over the places I've never been to and won't ever be, while my head is the only thing remaining, dethinking itself in all that hadn't been and won't ever be.

I began to write his name as dryly

as our ending

I loved so much

so often, so hard

maybe that's why I feel

so all over the place

swimming in the deep

souls

lost and found

within the event horizon

on any day

no goodbye is forever

Venus

You are the sum of your loving.

"Real love," said the old carpenter to the young lady,
"is a cock-and-bull story,
told by an idiot."

"But why," she answered,
"are you talking in those harsh, black-woven words?
You need to believe that one day you will see the light.
Maybe this nightmare you've pierced inside your head
is only a dream."

I swam in the open seas
and a faceless man counted the time
that nevermore belongs to me.

Do you feel the same?
Do you dream of a time
that bears another name?

You drew me in your own image
and I wrote your name all over my heart –
fiery lights are all I see behind my eyes.

choking on butterflies

I want a man who can provide me

      –   a secure place in his heart

      –   honour and respect for his and my self and us

he lets me be
the woman created in my own image

he lets us be
the symbiotic manifestation
of the vow
of fidelity
and faith
in a forever renewed happiness

a heart of gold makes a prince
not a golden wallet

the first time she met him
her heart pounded
up to her eyebrows

all of these thoughts I cannot send your way
which my heart passes to me in all of these hours
vibrate in all of my rooms
with a never-ending echo

it steals my speech, my sense
the fading of all words
your heart
and every speechless moment

some beauty shines so brightly

it blinds your eyes

What is it like to fall in love?

What does it feel like? It's this tingling sensation you feel, somewhere in the remotest corners of your stomach. The feeling that butterflies are dancing within you. The feeling that you never want to sleep again because reality finally feels better than any dream you've dreamt before. The feeling that all the colours all around you radiate a bit more than they did before and that your own radiance competes with all the colours all around you. The feeling that all the people all around you drink in this radiance, giving it back to you and that everything is ablaze with light and that everything fell into place and that everything will stay in this place. The feeling that your own happiness is intertwined with this significant other who suddenly found his way into your life. The feeling you feel within you whenever this significant other looks at you in this way, he doesn't look at anyone else. The feeling that you have already known this significant other for ages. The feeling that you waited for this significant other all your life. The feeling that you want to spend the rest of your days with this significant other. The feeling that you're not solely yourself and him not solely himself but that what has changed is bearing a name: we. We, together.

"You are the quintessence of beauty,"

he said

and her heart stood still.

Reason off.

Heart on.

you look like a painting

and on your left arm

you wear timelessness

no hyperbole lives up to you

Of quantum foam and shell tesseracts

D: „In the house of my childhood days, we had a shell that we had found in Portugal. It was really huge, and when you held it to your ear, you were able to listen to the sound of the sea. I loved that shell so much. I think that it's still at my daddy's place."

T: „The shells with the sound of the sea, I loved them as well! When I was a child, I always thought that molecular particles of the sea were saved inside of them or that its sound waves endlessly reflected inside of them."

D: „I thought the same. That the sea was saved inside these shells or that the concept of the sea lingered inside of them. And by saying that molecular particles were saved inside of them, maybe they could be named as shell tesseracts."

T: „That's the quantum foam. It saves the layers inside of them. As you know, two quanta are always interconnected, no matter how far the distance. By touching the former, you also touch the latter, whether they are near or far. And it's the same with the quanta within the shell. And it's the same with the quanta between us."

waking and dreaming

beholding the wonders before my eyes

mindlessly walking on clouds

and spellbound by your sight

Since I met you, I listen to Puccini from within.

The paper I write upon
is more patient than I will ever be
and never worth the thoughts
I let rain upon it.

They are too precious for me –
and so are you.

you move me in the sweetest of hours
your eyes like faraway lands
carry me to the edge of my world

and after all that comes to pass
I breathe in
the fragrance of change

love is a powerful force

I travelled a thousand seas
yet I haven't found a soul as golden
as yours

together we can shed light upon
a thousand worlds

aeons ago I wandered

over a grassless earth

in hidden worlds

I found the wonder

bearing your name

a voice as clear as daylight

He stated that he didn't want to travel to Paris:
"That's where love resides."

Her words were only a whisper –
a blushing:

"Then pick the girl
who might give space to this idea
and take her with you ..."

you're hours and miles away
and yet so close

with words, you draw a visible force

onto my mind

you're in the future

I'm in the past

and still, we're in the same place

strangeness and charms you're falling for –
for which you risk a second glance
you won't regret

in slow motion, I see my arrival
in your arms

we steal an idea of eternity
from this very moment

"Why do you take a photo of me?"

-

"Because you're beautiful."

they live in a different state –

a state of mind

you elusively sweet entity

I will gift you with kisses

sweeter than cake

softer than the morning dew

on flowers in the early light of day

within my scarlet dreams

the mountains catch fire

let's set fire

to our morning skies

and a sound like a storm passed us by

and I longed for the prime of the day

and your fresh dew upon my bloom

craving for higher heights
melting in your
geographical symphony
and my physical epiphany

play my heartstrings
enter my solar
let me serve you

I want to make love
to your brain

a fine frenzy can't keep the silence inside of me

you created an empty space

only you can balance

a hundred suns inside her body

longing for his crescent moon

heaven and earth
embrace and entwine
wander through valleys
and undulating lands

let us explore
uncover every corner
vulnerable nevermore

let us marvel at the wonder
that we are

skin like sunlight
and honeyed lips

he tastes like orange juice

and summer sunsets

like Italian wine

and Sunday afternoons

eyes of amber

and golden autumn days

like fragrant earth

and clearing rain

he works magic with his hands
drawing pictures on my skin
I can feel with my whole being
until the breaking of the day

I'll keep the memories on my skin
like trophies

your kisses are treasures
all the world shall see

fill me within my moon

on the surface of your sky

a crescent moon hangs up high

above the clouds veiling the sky

beneath the last dream of the setting sun

when I and the heavens were wrapped in flames

beyond all the words I wander
dawning and waking
light and dark

here my entire being longs for
beauty, truth and you

we are the ones
who walk the clouds

I search for the word soaring inside of me
weaving bashful dreams within –
a thought living a secret life:

how you read in all my souls
and still pour yourself into my life
seeing us in our entirety

meet me
in your dreams
my love
where the night ends
and the day begins

All the words we read have as much meaning as we grant them to have

The beginning.

A red bench by the beach.

Blue.

Flowers.

The room-divider.

Dreams made of paper.

I am alone.

The temple.

Sweetest life.

Him.

Ruby-red.

Foam of stars.

Flowers on the ground.

Rings.

Being together.

Sunlight.

The image of us is but a shadow.

Warm cold heart.

Snow.

Icy cold.

Death from freezing.

Leaves blown away in the wind.

Tristesse.

Eternity is but a pack of lies.

Black.

I choke.

Complementary corn roses.

A flight.

Look at the light; look at your life.

Footprints in the sand.

A single white dove.

Me, glancing out of the window in a hotel room in Paris.

A self-portrait:

full lips, light dress, dark mind.

Hope.

7 birds float in a breeze.

A dress gone with the wind.

Hands intertwine.

Freedom.

Time.

You.

pieces of her heart
showering over his head
like confetti

the moment I met you
I knew that you'd be my now or never

I'll give my life, I'll be your wife
I'll share with you the present
I'll gift you my forever

Love takes courage.

It's me, the robber's daughter –
you're the fearless prince.
There's no need to steal my heart,
for it's you who wins.

Like an open book

I long to tell you the story of my whole life.
I want to show you my innermost like an open book so that
you can read it.
Anything that you want.

I want to be perceivable and ... that you can perceive me.
I want to be comprehensible, like a mathematical formula
you can solve, even if I cannot solve myself.

I long for you to solve me. I long for you to read me like an
open book.
Anything that you want.

[...]

I long for you to tell me the story of your whole life.
I want you to show your innermost like an open book, so
that I can read it.
Anything that I want.
I want to make you perceivable and ... that I can perceive
you.

I want to make you comprehensible, like a mathematical formula I can solve, even if you cannot solve yourself.

I long for us to be solvable. That we show each other our innermost, like an open book.
Anything that we have ever wanted.

I turn the pages

and everywhere

I read your name

I awoke

in my repeating dreams of you:

days of sweetness

nights of music

for today and tomorrow

belong to us

time is the most precious thing I can give to you

because you and I are shaped by our finitude

but every finitude can grow ad infinitum

his past might not belong to me

but my future is his to keep

I was made for you

and you for me.

You're an extension of my being

and thus not strange to me – you never were.

How could I not have loved you from the beginning?

You're the completion

of my completeness.

the greatest love story

was ours to write

flowing in gold spun thread
she saw his innermost
and myriads of birds
whispered their secrets to them
at twilight time

A bird singing a silent song
amidst her heart
speaking this solitary truth –
a request so noble:

"Doesn't life live amidst hope?
Come and stay with me –
if my heart belongs to someone
this someone will be you."

while looking in your eyes

the whole world seems understandable

for me

you make me feel more real

whenever my thoughts

go on your journey

stars are born within me

you look into my eyes

you see your dream within my own

all the days and always

you carry my heart within your own

all my sunsets

and moonlit skies

belong to you

kiss me beneath the starlit skies
I want to dance with you
through the beginning
to the very end

the heat, the dust, the colours,
the words, the memories,
I can't feel them without you

if I was a dream
I'd want to be yours

forever my loveliest, you shall be more kind to me

than the adornment of the moon

ablaze in the infinite night

a blaze igniting my song

and if the shadowy creatures

want to gain upon me

you are my insouciance

my zero gravity

in all the gravity

within and all around me

I have always stampeded
yet my feet had never longed for
what my heart had desired

I heard all of your thoughts float within me
and every breath of air that carried love to me
and your heart that carried every new second

I am the sand under your feet
and you carry me away
with paper, flowers and dreamy hands

and even if one day I might be all alone again
I wouldn't be lonely
but blessed
with all the memories of you

if time is blown away in the wind
I want it to take me back to you

I love you with my entire soul
drowsy and wary and dark and light

oh! dost thou know

yer art of radiant beauty

thy beauty shines

and shimmers in thy soul

I lay my head on his shoulder
and above me, I saw the amber leaves
passing by against the bright blue sky
on the day when all the burdens fell from my shoulder
the sun was much too warm
for a day in mid-October
and even the senses were warm

my light resides in all your shades –
I write your hidden self on every page
of my now that no one has ever known before

your ghost draws itself on all my tongues
solely speaking your language

uncompromisingness and devotion

is the quintessence of love

to give everything and expect nothing

and be blessed with all

you never dared to dream about

because it's mutual

and softly you write yourself on my soul

and transform it into the paper

not-to-be-forgotten

the smallest of gestures mirror the greatest of feelings

Moments

And even after all these days, I still find the sand in my shoes and on the floor, and I want to pick up every single grain of sand with my hands and feel them because all of them are a memento of you.

And even after all these days, this feeling is still as present as in the moments when your touch left its mark on my skin.

And even after all these days I think back to the kisses you stole from me and when I lay in your arms and the both of us looked into this nightly sky that didn't darken completely and always shone with this soft violet glow at the horizon and when the ships transformed into surreal points of light, like stars that fell from the sky and when I realized that this moment belongs entirely to us and that I want to belong entirely to you.

Every morning is a beginning,
every evening a farewell.
The everlasting resurgence lets me start anew –
I will enshrine every tear, every smile.
None of it I will let go or die.

Never will I forget ...

My confessions have always been
words full of deceit –
a house built on sand.

[...] I planted a flower in your garden.
We enshrine an eternity
not to be found in any reality.

You are the dome of my sky and my soil.
In your shadow I can thrive –
it gives the only light
that lets me live.

... I see your coming and going –
but my heart leans on your resurgence.

time and again I'll return

to the magic of the moment

I first laid my eyes upon yours

in the awakening landscape

the arising dawn

she floats in rose-coloured skies

breezing through drowsy greenery

I will plant the seeds of our love in a garden

shower it with kisses

and bright sunlight

and it will forever grow

he made my soul blossom

until my heart stood in full bloom

so I guess he transformed me

into a flower

An everlasting garden

I gift you the forget-me-not and the lavender in my garden,
fresh tastes of the trampolining bees. Even the pink-
coloured, large-leaved flowers standing firmly together,
whose name slipped my mind or had never even come across
it.
The magnolia tree that had fragrantly heralded the early
spring and which we passed by – hand in hand.
All the arbours overgrown with millionfold roses I haven't
yet promenaded with you.
And the wisteria that dripped from the summery walls like
rain.
All the colourful leaves the trees take off when the days grow
colder.
All the dahlias we will plant when my house becomes yours.
A green and gaily coloured bouquet to tell you all the things
I'm not able to put into words.

if love was a tree
I'd plant you a forest

he could neither be like the rain
nor like cloud-coloured skies

his heaven filled with infinite suns
shining in the sweetest shades of gold and blue

his shape as beautiful as a never-ending summer

and in our hearts there had always resided
the truth that told
that we were meant to be

In the unknown lands

in the unknown lands, unleashed, unburdened
we built a whole new world
with these hands of thine and mine

it's our reality that lives and grows on me
nothing will die or pass, shall be forgotten
these moments oh so full of you

we forget ourselves in the present
all that was past is past
what it will be doesn't matter
when I lay myself in your hands

nevermore passing
in a long-lost reality of my own self
with this flattering smile
that draws itself
upon these lips of mine

you are the light in my shade

you carry me through the dark

you take away the shadows of my every day

and enlighten my existence

the days of dread are over

now let me be your happiness

a relationship doesn't mean

"being as free as before"

it means to dedicate yourself

to become a part of a greater whole

it means experience:

to recognize your own self within the other one

it means completion:

to feel another, more complete kind

of freedom

I feel your thoughts
as if they were mine

and no matter how often I
lost myself in others
I'll always find myself in you

no legions can conquer me
he rules the realm of my heart

Arrival

"Your voice makes me calm down," he said drowsily.

He lay beside her in bed, rolled up in her arms. She felt his breath upon her chest.

She ran her fingers through his thick and curly hair and smiled.

"That's quite cheesy, you know that?"

"Mmh," he mumbled, just about to fall asleep.

Skin nestled to the skin, and she wouldn't have wanted to be anywhere else but here.

Arrival - did it feel like that?

you are the arrival and the journey

always new, yet familiar

your arms are my home

Together everything will get better

I step out onto the balcony. The second glass of the French
white wine I bought at the tiny station with the two tracks
feels warm inside my belly. The ten-pointed star of the guest
house from across the street shines in the descending
nightfall. It's 9pm. The cake was well-received, you said.
Thanks, you said. For the idea and for the realization. And
yet we have realized it together. And because of these small
loving signs of appreciation, I love you even more than I
already do. And I miss you. All of this beauty all around me
– all the lush green meadows, all the massive walls of rock,
all the greenery in all of its various shades and all the half-
timbered houses – they all are just half as beautiful without
you. And the bed is too soft, and the pillow is too
comfortable to lie on it all by myself.
"A doll's bed," you would say once again. Made for a single
person. Yet still, I wish you were here. You would fit in here.
Just as you did five months and a day ago. That's when we
started to exist. And I don't want to spend a single day
without this certainty anymore that warms my belly. Even
without French white wine.

a house full of books

music and love

there: me and you

the thieves of words

Do you really need that much to be happy?

The house made of sandstones is located at the end of the street. Three sheep are browsing in the garden. Five chicken with their fluffy feathering are picking grains from the ground. The hydrangeas keep watch around the white-lacquered garden fence.

They aren't tired yet, and neither am I. And they still are warm and fragrant from the ceasing summer.

Moments ago, I waved goodbye to the island in the sea that had grown out of the peppercorn of a giant, hundreds of years ago, and the city that a monk dedicated to an archangel who had visited him once upon a dream.

The air is mild and salty.

Tomorrow we will meet again, and I will wait for you at the pyramid.

[...]

The city is big and hectic and unnecessary for our happiness. You're holding me in your arms. I don't need more. We dance to *Madeleine Peyroux* and the song that became ours, as so many had before.

„I belong to you. I have belonged to you for years. You pleaded for tolerance. You were the only one who did.

You were beautiful and courageous, and I haven't found the courage to talk to you. Do you remember?"

Every occurrence in our lives makes sense. And it made sense that we found each other, yet parted, but without forgetting.

Outside, the golden heart glistens in the beams of sunlight that make their way through the clouds. It's warm, just like our senses.

Then I notice that tears fall on my shoulder.

"Why are you crying," I ask you, clasped in my arms.

"For joy," you answer.

I will hold you in my arms.

Our big day will come, and I will dance with you. And if you cry, we will cry together.

And if we laugh, we will laugh together.

I will dance with you until my legs can dance no more.

I will gift you every day I wake.

And if we wake no more, I will search you at the place we go to when our souls dissolve into their atomic units.

As we always did.

we might not be perfect

but perfect for one another

an autumn eve –

the wind is bitter cold

but I'm not cold

for I have you to warm my heart

you are the dream
I never dared to dream
too good to be true
with eyes like rain
you dry all the tears
of my bygone days

your mouth is a beam of sunlight
lightening up each of my days
a prince without a steed
but with a heart of gold
for a princess
without a kingdom or a home

the crown upon your pate
invisible for so many pairs of eyes –
past fate
passed you to me

I see you and your noble soul
and all of your thoughts are felt
as mine and ours

we find each other in every lifetime
the present, the past
within no age of life shall be oblivion
even without recollection –
we'll find each other forevermore

those who have found each other once
will find each other again and yet again

.

Mars

not is not a place
I want to travel to

I want this life
to be much more than
a "death will befall us all"

I want to fill it
with sweet significance

a raison d'être
for being under the sun

I don't want to confine myself to what-if's
I want to be bold & brave

running with the wolves

through dark forbidden forests

and magic woven words

all that blooms

must wither first

summer slumbered in hidden buds
and its warmth was a promise
of roses soon-to-be

hidden sleep
through promises of long-gone days –
I missed you even when I had you around

natures of heart and heaven
aided me through the storm of my soul –
in millennial forests, our destinies intertwined

autumn comes nigh with footsteps oh so soft
the sun is low on the heaven's tent
leaves transform into liquid gold
trees lay themselves to rest
all is awake, and nothing will die
every farewell is a longing reunion –
every ending a beginning

storms carry me into every distance –
beyond the places I know by heart
I stay and wait

We write.
We open ourselves –
carry ourselves from the inside out.

We – the wanderers of reality.
Working on wonders.
Weaving the words.
Fulfilling the truth.

Wandering in welters
in words on the water –
wistfulness and delight within.

Goals, goals, goals ... You talk as if life were a competition.

only by conquering the past
you can appreciate the future

Those who do not know emotional baggage also do not
know about the tribulations of the world.
But those who do not learn to cope with its burdens also
forget about its beauty.

we have to live everything –
the good and the bad

A pop of colour can frighten away the grey

Do you know these days? These days when the alarm rings, and there's no energy left to get up because you think that today nothing will change and nothing good will happen anyway?
I had that feeling when I woke up this morning. The dream I had dreamt passed into the next day without any transition, and I cried myself awake. The alarm rang. I felt horrible, and I didn't know where I was. My dreams have always been very vivid, very real – it can be a blessing and a curse. Today it had been a curse.

Usually, you cry yourself to sleep – but on particular days, you cry yourself awake. Years ago, which I can count on the fingers of both of my hands, I would have felt very much at home in this feeling. I would have wallowed in it. Melancholy had been my very best friend for oh so many years. But it's not like that anymore. Life is radiant and colourful. Even though there are days that seem dull and grey. But even those days will pass.

Joy is an active choice. Sometimes you have to even fight for it. But one day, you will be richly gifted.

Then you will gain something that weighs more than all the loneliness, the guilt, the sadness:
pure life.

Some time ago, I consciously decided against surrendering to the grey within me. And I promised myself to leave my bed every day, even on the days that seemed dull and grey, and to throw myself into the day the same way I wanted to throw myself into life.
Life is the only thing we can call our very own.
And if the grey appears to be too grey, one has to show one's true colours.
Inside and out.

And that's why I wear red because a pop of colour can frighten away the grey.

if you're having a bad day

dress as if it might become your best

if you don't take your time
you will never have it

the wrong ones come to leave
the right ones come to stay

I never learned to hate anyone
and I won't change it for you

What Paris means to me

Arrival. Abscission.

Nearness. Distance.

Dazzling, mesmerizing beauty. Enchantment. Amazement.

Anxiety. Grief. Hatred.

Fatigue.

Lust and Love.

Cigarettes and Music.

Strangeness and Charms.

The red and the black.

Life and death.

Everything.

culture is pigeon-holing –
it disposes of the world
yet takes away its freedom

waking up is what I wish for the world
so that it can keep on turning

the only race you have to run
is with yourself

Even in hope, there is fear

Hope believes that everything will turn out right in the end,
but always with a touch of fear.
Hope isn't knowledge. It isn't a certainty.
Hope proves nothing – one must do.
One must act to transform hope into certainty, which
conquers the fear within it.

at the station

dreams are dying

hopes are born

„Tag along! Tag along!"

that's what happiness is calling

but many cannot catch up with it

I will run on

as far as my feet will carry me

It takes a whole life to become young again

Age is merely a numeric concept. It tells us nothing about
wisdom, the nature of the soul, or life experiences.
The physically young can feel like the old and the old can
move through life with a light-hearted, childlike nature.

The scars of time often are not visible from the outside. At
times you can encounter a seemingly young girl who
ingested life as a concentrate and who had non-visibly aged
in a time-lapse.

A lot of things can go awry in your life.
And the world owns a lot of possibilities to let you suffer.
Living isn't for the faint-hearted. Ageing isn't as well.
Therefore it takes a lot of strength to make the walls
collapse, to find the way back to the surface, to leave
hopelessness behind.

To accept and cherish life, to understand its concept, might
be a lifelong task. It might take ages, but it is possible. For
each and every individual. No matter what you had to go
through.

My best time

My mother always spoke of a "flowering period" of each and every human being in which his or her true beauty comes to light – from the inside and the outside.

I didn't have it in the past.

I look at old photographs and think: "Darling, that hasn't been you. That has been you on the way to your own self, but still lightyears away."

Meanwhile, I am more myself than I could have been in the past.

Small steps can change the world.

Why don't we just start to honestly answer the question of how we are feeling?
Why don't we just start to give up our standards and make room for the truth of our humanity?

Emotions make us human. Without being able to feel something, we cannot be anything more than machines.

Giving up is not an option

It's up to you to find joy in your life. Don't let yourself be stylized as a victim.
You're able to pull the strings, even if things couldn't get any worse. To realize that can be difficult, and at times it might take an outside person to make that clear.
There's always a way out and ...
Giving up is no escape and no option.

Success is made of 1% of luck and 99% of sweat.

Sometimes you find yourself in the obvious outland

In his books, Marcel Proust described how scents and
odours can make people recall other situations, other times,
other people.
They cause a feeling of home and arrival in the obvious
outland and remoteness.

You're not old until you don't try something new.

Read as much as you can –
knowledge is the most essential luggage
to carry through your life
and it doesn't weigh anything at all.

Books are gifts. They nourish your mind, spirit, and heart.

How do you encounter the stones that life is throwing your way?

The end of an era marks the beginning of a new.
Consider challenges as chances. To grow. To build. To live.
For the better. To create something great, you wouldn't have imagined in advance.

There are no such things as bad experiences. There are only possibilities to learn.

Take risks. Throw away the doubts. You're young. Your whole life, it's all ahead of you, even though you like to let yourself be told otherwise, preferably from yourself. All the months of May you've already lived are nothing compared to how you're perceived or to how you feel. You're young. You're allowed to make mistakes: so be brave and make mistakes! Cast away your doubts and take the chances that spin around your head like satellites even though you like to tell yourself otherwise.

For years I had been reducing my own personal stone.
Sometimes bigger, sometimes smaller pieces of it.
The more I reduced, the more freely I could breathe.

To reduce the bits and pieces of stone, I consciously decided to put myself into situations that were strange and new for me.

Often even situations that scared me.

At the end of May, I decided to take a step that would change my life. I realized that the stone inside of me still had too much of a hold on me, and I couldn't and wouldn't stand that any longer.

It was a watershed.

Deep down inside, I knew that I would regret it if I didn't take my chance. But if I hadn't had people around me who would have reaffirmed and encouraged me in this thinking, I would never have followed the path of this thought inside of me. I wouldn't have chosen risk over safety. But I did and thus ...

I have found myself.

It's amusing that you sometimes need a stranger to help you to become yourself again.

Be someone you'd like to know yourself.

conservative but liberal

thoughtful but courageous

I'm drawn into the distance

far from the well-known

reviving my spirits

to find my own happiness

Sometimes you have to burn something old to create something new

It can be healing to let go of the old. What that letting go will look like everybody has to decide on one's own. Most people however decide, year by year, to let go of the old with a loud bang and a multitude of firecrackers and pyrotechnics.
I decided on a different way. Quiet. Attentive. Reflective.
To let go of everything I wanted to let go.
All of which I didn't want to carry with me into the next year.
It ought to be warm.
In the shades of red, orange & yellow.

All the negative thoughts that had burdened my heart and hadn't let my soul come to rest, I cast into the flames.

Rituals of any kind have a lot of liberating energy. They can have a holistic and extremely positive influence on your state of mind.
When I wrote down all the dreadful and sad thoughts and memories that still had an impact on my whole being and afterwards gave them to the flames, I was able to experience

that feeling of liberating energy myself.

And it had also been a symbolic act, choosing the path of the fire as the source of purification - in my early childhood, it had been the element I had feared most (because I had fallen into the bonfire once).

To let go of my fears and my grief in this way felt very cathartic because, in this way, I was also able to reflect on this primal fear and to let go of it as well.

Contemplation prevents pain.

Becoming aware of the things you were never able to endure makes you realize what you don't want to endure anymore.

Everything that had been difficult and that's still difficult will pass. Other things will cross your path that are difficult. But there's no need to be afraid.

Life has its highs and lows. That's the nature of things.

Overcoming obstacles makes us stronger.

It makes us stronger to master new obstacles, which again grant us the chance to become stronger.

It grants us the possibility to become better and better versions of our selves.

It grants us the possibility to experience the strength that dwells within us.

It grants us the possibility to feel our strength and our pride in times of darkness.

We have to be ready to live all of this and to fill it with life. It's worth it.

We only live once on this planet we call our home in this present condition and consciousness, and that makes it so incredibly precious.

There's only now, not later.

Your life longs to be lived - after all, it's your only one.

And thus we cannot procrastinate to do precisely that:

to live.

There's always room for change.

Change your mind. Change your life.

It is not granted to us that what we wish for most of all will fall into our laps. Luck is no star-money falling into our laps when we stupidly stare into the starry skies and wait for something to happen. No.
We have to actively participate in searching for and creating our very own happiness.

In the Declaration of Independence, the pursuit of happiness is mentioned – it is one of the fundamental rights of every human being, as well as freedom and life itself. We cannot passively *expect*. We have to actively *strive* for it.

Every human can change his life for the better if he is willing to take the heat for it.
But it takes courage.

courage is the key to open every door

You only live once – why would you want to be a projection of other people's perceptions?

to travel is essential
to grasp the world
but you don't need
to travel the world
to grasp yourself

The only valuable acknowledgement is the acknowledgement you grant yourself.

The only person you have to answer to about your doing and your becoming is your own self.

Be your own idol.

I wouldn't want to be
what I don't say aloud
no stories that speak me
in a me, that doesn't exist

at times I do not think
yet I can think
yet I can be a thought
at times I am not present
yet I don't lose my presence

without a soul, I'm still a body
without a body still a soul

never altogether gone
forevermore the only one
who lasts in every day

nothing is impossible
except for the things we do not do

we are the transformed

we are the awoken

we lay your visions of a concrete world

in ashes

we build a new, a living world

away from death and decay

Jupiter

I sketch my life
as my own, my entirety
as the only true love
the only true magic

If you were a painting, what would it look like?

If there was a soul, where would it reside?

What makes you feel alive?

my darling girl –

if only you knew
which wondrous turns
life has in store for you

omnipresence
irrational poetics
circular perfection
therein the entire world
therein the entire universe

shoot for the moon

aim for the stars

Your freedom begins where you stop doing what the others expect from you.

within the depths of my soul
renewal was born
towards joy and my beating heart
for it is predestined

Friends are family we have chosen ourselves.

Dearest child, soulful entity, weaver of words, sister of my heart –

you chime with the song of the Maybird within you
you carry every summer sunbeam in your heart
you dance with the play of colours in all the autumn treetops
only you can bear the winter crystals
when my heart is in danger to freeze to death
and keep me warm

and if you can't be strong
I can be your strength

misty beings shall nevermore cross your path
only golden glimmer shall reside in the spaces of your soul
blackness shall fade away from your depths
knowledge of your glory shall be alive within you

pretty darling, don't you dare
to doubt your golden soul
in your entire soulfulness
you are already whole

where do the bees go
when they go to sleep

you're wearing spring
wandering through this whole new world
awakening in dreams never dreamt nor felt

your cheeks are peonies in their first sweet bloom
your lips wear roses dressed in scarlet -
as velvety and sweet as your heart

world not awoken

a millionfold blooming stars

invisible for a world in dreams

the first morning bird sings

a faint-hearted song

for an insomniac girl

The tragedy in life is never tragic as a whole

Sometimes the path that leads to finding your very own self leads across the heart of another person. And when the time has come, you have to let him go, because some people are your preterite.

Don't indulge yourself in reminiscences of the past. There's always a reason why things happen the way they do. And if something old is dying, something new will be born.

The present is the only thing that matters. It's the only thing that really exists.
The past shouldn't be a part of it. It belongs to us, as all the things that we have experienced, suffered, learned, but it should never affect our present.

The only thing we can form is what is present. And this present is the most valuable property we own.
And we must make use of this present. We must cherish it.

And I fill my present with dreams of fairytale castles and walks in the sun that is getting warmer on every new day.
I fill it with dreams of glances onto the lavish splendour of

rose-coloured spring and summer blossoms, of new poetry and new songs, of melodies in my heart and kindred souls, of new colours on my skin and flights through strange yet familiar worlds and the ever anew and ever perpetuating abundance and magic of life.

Because the tragedy in life is never tragic as a whole. It grants us the chance to be more than what we have been before.

the past doesn't define me

I define myself through my present self

find someone who embraces your light

yet doesn't fear your darkness

a stubborn heart will always find a way

to pick up all the stars from all the skies

it's dreaming of

It has been real, it will always stay real

All the people we have ever loved remain. They are our
ghosts. They make us who we are now.
Everyone stays. And that's alright.

If you have found the right thing, the old ghost will let you
go – it will not haunt you.
This is the miracle: that everything is possible – despite
everything.

I have loved so many different people. Maybe that's why I
feel so all over the place.
It doesn't pass – it will never pass.
It has been real; it will always stay real.
But that doesn't mean that it has to haunt you.
You might believe that the old ghost had been the big
picture, but he might solely have been the preparation for
the bigger picture.

Everything is possible because the universe is as vast and
infinite as the human heart.

Let the world in. Fate wishes us well.

Who knows which worlds will reveal themselves to us.
Believe in wonders, and they will come to pass.

if we start creating our own lives
the true magic happens

The virtuoso isn't always the one who has his métier down to a fine art but the one who lives for it.

in music, I have always been
different from my inner being –
feeling free and living aloud
it had been my hidden truth

Music is a feeling I cannot put down in words.

I see music.

I feel it in every fibre of my body and every part of my soul.

A harmony that touches my soul can release torrents within me and shake me to the very foundations, make me remember the good and the bad, hope, and despair.

Makes me dark and makes me light.

I want to be a never-ending melody.

I listened to *Broken Parable* by *Bears Den,* and I thought of you, and for the umpteenth time, I had been surprised at how well song lyrics could put the feelings that you feel at this very moment in words. I thought of the soundtrack of the indie game *To the Moon* and the song *Everything's Alright* by *Laura Shirigaya*, which mirrored the sentiment so perfectly that I had felt when the wall had been between us, although it had only been for a short time. On Tuesday - do you remember?

And I thought about how much a soundtrack could capture me, making me want to relisten and rewatch the credits over and over again to inject it into me - all this emotion.

To preserve all that flared inside of me.

To make me aware of the symbiosis of the visual and musical and to never let it go again.

All of which I also wanted in my own life.

Music – I know my dreams within you.

I see you within me.

Music – I behold you.

I see you dancing with all the colours I carry within me.

When melodies make their way through the air

I feel you in all of my fibres and pores.

Music – only you infuse the deepest depths of my soul.

Make me move on to pastures new

and new shapes of my soul –

you make me safe and sound.

music was my first love

but it won't be my last

Life has to be danced

Dancing is my passion. Dancing means dreaming with your feet. The poetry of your body. What I cannot express with words I express with my body. I move to the music, let it flow through my limbs. Form the notes within me. Make them visible. Become one with the music. I become an instrument. I become music. I am music. I am entirely in the moment. I live and breathe and swirl in a circle, flow in gentle movements with the harmonies, fly through the skies. I am all mine, all my own. I am free.

dancing makes your soul grow
its own pair of wings

The irreversibility of our fate

I still remember that moment, years ago, when someone I dearly loved had to die a tragic death. And I thought about all the beloved people in my life and sensed a feeling of fear, of losing them one day, because, in the end, we'll lose everyone we have ever loved, no matter how. And I thought that nothing in this world is meant to last and that nothing is going to stay forever. But then I also realized that ... it doesn't need to stay. It's here now. It's felt now. And drifting apart and breaking up and having to die are such things that belong to life. And without death, no living thing can exist. It is our fate to one day crumble into dust ... and it is and always will be a painful and cruel experience, to lose someone you loved with the whole of your heart. But this is also what makes life so unique. This is what makes it meaningful. This is what makes it so unbelievably precious. This is why you should live every day as if it was your last one. This is why you shouldn't hide away your feelings from those people your heart belongs to. This is why you should tell them what you feel. Always. This is why you should listen to your heart and never stop listening. This is why you should give your all and love and love and love and love.

life doesn't belong to us –
we belong to life

belong to it since the beginning
until the end of time

Life is our childhood, and death is the beginning of our
immortality.

Omnipresence

In can feel God in everything, but especially in nature.
But man needed to have a place to see the Lord, and thus
the churches were built. It started with Solomon's temple so
that the ark of the covenant had a place of quiet and rest, as
well as the Israelites.

I love churches – those places of encounter, exchange,
community, and kindred spirits. But nonetheless, God
shines the brightest in nature, and it's manifold beauty.
He is everywhere.

God is love. And if you feel love for another person, the
revelation of God is revealed in its most beautiful way – it
resembles the beauty of a flower or the swelling and swaying
of a willow tree.

Christian faith is gentle and kind.
It is full of hope and love and tolerance for all the people
wandering this earth.
That's what I believe in, and that's what I have experienced.

I want to dare to believe so much more
to tell Him all that he means to me
nevermore despairing in this faith
to raise my prayers up to Him

I want to take a glance upon heaven and earth
the worldly, the otherworldly
the profane, mundane, the sacred
the fragments that have stolen my heart

Life is the never-ending story of searching for beauty.

wildly romantic wandering
over new earth, new worlds
bearing the heralds of spring
to hold them dear

be a wildflower
amongst cut flowers

coffee, sunsets, flowers, and kisses
the simple joys are the sweetest

she walks over honeyed ground
wildflowers blooming all over her

allow yourself to grow

Clouds add character to the heavens.

I have wandered restlessly
Through the worlds - leaving no trace
Searching for some wholesomeness
Or what they would call happiness

But I cannot catch a glimpse
of what I search until I see:
That what I yearned to find
it has always been there inside of me

Wandering through the dark
I felt my soul arise
And in my heart, I felt a spark
Ignite

„Where do our dreams go when we're no longer sleeping?“

-

„On paper,

if it lies beside you when you wake up.

Or they live on

in our thoughts.“

It's good to have dreams because they remind us of all the things possible.

Don't search.

Let yourself be found.

every dream becomes a wish

when called by its name

and every wish has a chance

to be fulfilled

dreams are realities

a word in flight and fire and finery

a roundel written on infinite pages

a world created out of everything and nothing

arisen from fruitful glory

a word was born out of sorrow

to meet joy and life

giving the truth, forming the new

gifting me my very own self

The impossible becomes a reality through our written words.

in the turning of the tides, she crosses the seas
her pen children wear new garments
they levitate in the new heavens –
a kaleidoscope of possibilities

she read a whole new world
in the setting sun

it's autumn in the summer sun
and winter in the shade
I'm thinking back to days in Paris
where all my dreams were made

the red city is visible heat
even with your eyes closed
you can surmise its spectrum

If it feels right, it cannot be wrong.

I love photography because it preserves the moment.

what we can see from here

is so much more

then what we could have dreamt of

All I want is everything.

Embrace the moment and feel alive

Have you ever had that feeling that you're completely in this very moment, now, living, breathing, there with your whole being?

I'm sitting on the hump of the Arabian camel. I feel the warm wind flowing around me like a never-ending stream. It's 48 degrees. I feel the heat on my skin, behold the endless, weightless, sandy open, and sense that I have fully arrived at this very moment. I'm here. I'm now. I'm alive. It is an incredible feeling, an incredibly full feeling of freedom and self-love, and love for the world, and I realize that everything is possible. I see the retrospective of my whole sensitivity, the odyssey of my life, my depression, my suffering, and loving until I have finally been able to arrive in this perfect marvellous moment, and I feel free. Simply free. Boundless and free.

The first time I had that feeling that I'm totally present at this very moment had been at the age of fifteen when I read *The Solitaire Mystery* by *Jostein Gaarder*. A boy of fifteen years who travels the world with his father tells us the story of this feeling. He's lying in the loft bed. Above him, his father is snoring. It is night, and he cannot fall asleep because, in this very moment, he realizes that he's completely there, completely in this very moment, now, living, breathing, and marvelling at the miracle of his being. It's an overwhelming feeling.

But at the age of fifteen, I hadn't been free. I knew that I existed, but I felt as if trapped in a cage with nowhere to hide. I was trapped in the cage of my own feelings. The cage of my depression.

It had been an odyssey of many years into adulthood through trials and tribulations and self-inflicted and outward disappointments until I finally had been able to say that I can embrace the moment and feel alive. That I can be free. That I can be taken up at this very moment. That I love this life, I'm allowed to live.

The moment I ultimately realized that I have made it through all of the trials and tribulations and obstacles of my life's journey to finally see my own true self was while riding on an Arabian camel in the Sahara desert. With the warm wind flowing around me. With myself within me.

And that's also why I will never forget this journey and this country. And that's also why my love for this country is as vast and infinite as the Sahara desert.

And that's why I will return there. Again and again and
again. It is the place where I realized that I am free.
That I made it.
That everything, simply everything, is possible.

So many people live their lives without ever experiencing
something significant. Every day of their lives is the same.
And then, at the end of their life's journey, they wonder why
they cannot answer the question of whether they have lived
at all. Because they never felt present as a whole. But without
being wholly present and without the feeling of being
existent in the present, within one's own true self, and now,
one cannot know oneself, and one cannot recognize the
precious gift of life.
Because that's precisely what it is:
a gift.

You must create the life you want to live in.

I want to travel. I want to laugh. I want to live and love and be happy. I want to spend time with my favourite human beings. I want to dance and dance and dance. I want to encounter strangers as if they are friends I do not know yet. I want to see people like they really are. I want deep talk. I want depth. I want to swim through the dark waters in fearlessness. I want to let go of the anger, fear, and hatred that's still remaining in my heart. I want to have a pure soul, to speak only words of truth, and to live that truth in everything I think and feel and do. I want to show the people I love that I love them and oh, how I love them they ought to know. I want to show my own inner self. I want the world to see who I am. I want to show the colours, all the colours of my soul and my heart that got rid of all the blackness of the past. I want to be heartfelt emotion, and vulnerability, and strength. I want to be fearlessness. I want to be a rainbow. I want to be a golden queen. I want to be the maze you never ever want to leave. A fairy. A goddess. A woman.

I want to be real.

I embrace my own truth.

They always told me that my eyes mirrored the glamour and the gravity of the sea.
Why should I wonder at how much I can be myself whenever I am with her.

The people here are different.

They walk differently. Talk differently.

They are more considerable.

In the sequence of their steps, their countenances, their gestures, their words.

The people, the mood, and life itself ... walks at a slower pace.

But not the sea – it's rough, vivacious, tempestuous as it has always been.

Just like me, in the depths of my soul.

We are the living contradiction, the commotion, in a sea full of truth.

I'm proud of you

Five words. So simple. Yet we voice them all too rarely.
I'm proud of you. Of me. Of us. Of everything we are. Of
us, as the people we are.
Of everything we have already felt, learned, mastered.

What are you proud of?
And of whom?

„Mum, how do I spell home?“

-

„With your heart, my dear.“

all the suns within you

want to shine

be bold

be young

and curious

and courageous

and love and love and love

and never regret a day in your life

The present,

the presence:

a present.

About the author

Dahi Tamara Koch was born in Germany in 1988. Having lived in France and South Korea and travelling the world, she decided to move to her adopted home town Baden-Baden near the French border.

After studying Anglistics and Philosophy, she began to work as a private tutor and piano teacher.

Her love for writing became clear very early. At the age of twelve, her father bought her an antique typewriter on which she wrote her first short stories and poems.

At the age of nineteen, she published her first German poetry book. Three years later, her second book was published. The German version of „Within the event horizon" was published in 2019.

Since 2018 Dahi Tamara Koch has been publishing poetry and prose in English and German on her poetry blog @sie.ist on Instagram.

She is currently working on her first novel, which will be published later this year.